Spelling and Vocabulary

Dictionary

Author:

Mary Ellen Quint, Ph.D.

Editor:

Alan Christopherson, M.S.

Graphic Design:

Jennifer L. Davis, B.S.

Illustration:

Alpha Omega Creative Services

Alpha Omega Publications, Inc. • Rock Rapids, IA

©MMI by Alpha Omega Publications, Inc.®

804 N. 2nd Ave. E.
Rock Rapids, IA 51246-1759

Printed in the United States of America

ISBN 978-0-7403-0217-6

How to Use this Dictionary

The *Spelling Dictionary* is an integral part of the Horizons Spelling Program and accomplishes several purposes:

1. Students will become acquainted with the format and function of a simple dictionary.

2. Students will learn the function of guide words and diacritical markings.

3. Students will be able to see and read their spelling words within the context of a sentence.

4. Students will have an opportunity to practice their alphabetizing and reading/writing skills by using the *Spelling Dictionary* to perform the following tasks:

   ■ Look up the spelling words at the beginning of each week's lessons.

   ■ Record their weekly "Working Words" in the appropriate locations at the back of the Spelling Dictionary.

   ■ Use the *Spelling Dictionary* as a resource for writing sentences and stories.

Parts of speech are identified, and plural and comparative forms of words are also shown.

Pronunciation Guide

ă	ant, gas		ŏ	hot, pond
ā	ache, May		ō	go, poke
ä	tall, March		ô	fort, across
			oi	boy, enjoy
ĕ	let, yell		ou	how, mouth
ē	we, meek			
ėr	term, church		ŭ	hut, up
			u̇	full, book
ĭ	hit, lip		ü	rule, move
ī	ice, knife			

ə   a in across

e in taken

i in pencil

o in lemon

u in circus

Adapted from *Scott, Foresman Beginning Dictionary* by E.L. Thorndike/Clarence L. Barnhart, Scott, Foresman and Company, ©1988, 1983, 1979, 1976.

A

ache
(āk) *n.* a dull pain
Joe had an <u>ache</u> in his ankle.
plural: aches
v. having a dull pain
I <u>ache</u> all over after that fall.
ache, aches, ached, aching

across
(ə krôs′) *prep.* over, from one side to another
Judy and Paul ran <u>across</u> the field.

afternoon
(ăf′t ə r nün′) *n.* part of the day from noon to night
We will go swimming this <u>afternoon</u>.

airplane
(er′ plān) *n.* a machine used
to fly from place to place
The red <u>airplane</u> flew very
close to the ground.
Compound word: air + plane

along
(ə lông′) *prep.* follow a line or route from one place
to another
The boat sailed <u>along</u> the shore.

alphabet
(ăl′ f ə bet) *n.* series of letters used to make words
Can you write the <u>alphabet</u>?

ant
(ănt) *n.* small insect
An <u>ant</u> crawled across the table.

anyone   (ĕn′ ē wun) *pron.* any person whatever; anybody
Is <u>anyone</u> here from Chicago?
Compound word: any + one

April   (Ā′ prəl) *n.* the 4th month of the year
The flowers bloom in <u>April</u>.

around   (ə round′) *prep.* to surround or to encircle
Bill's father took a trip <u>around</u> the world.

ask   (ăsk) *v.* to question
Jesus said, "Whatever you <u>ask</u> the Father in my name, he will give."
ask, asks, asking, asked

asked   (ăskt) *v.* past tense of ask
Matt <u>asked</u> Max to eat with him.

August   (Ô′ gəst) *n.* the 8th month of the year
Jackie's birthday is in <u>August</u>.

aunt   (ănt) *n.* sister of your mother or father
Martha's <u>aunt</u> and uncle came to visit.

axes   (ăk′ səz) *n.* plural of *ax*
The <u>axes</u> used to chop the wood were sharp.

B

baby
(bā′ bē) *n.* a very young child or animal
When Bob was a <u>baby</u>, he liked ice cream.

bare
(ber) *adj.* empty, without covering
Because the cupboard was <u>bare</u>, Joe went shopping.

baseball
(bās′ bôl) *n.* (1) a game; (2) the ball used in the game of baseball
Dan likes to play <u>baseball</u> with his friends.
Compound word: base + ball

batter
(băt′ ər) *n.* a player who is hitting a ball with a bat
The third <u>batter</u> hit a home run.

bear
(ber) *n.* a large, furry mammal
A giant brown <u>bear</u> crossed the road in front of our car.

became
(bĭ kām′) *v.* past tense of *become*
The dog <u>became</u> very quiet after he ate.

become
(bĭ kŭm′) *v.* to grow or to be something
Our puppy will <u>become</u> a good guard dog someday.
become, becomes, becoming, became

bedroom
(bĕd rüm) *n.* place where one sleeps
Bob and Jim share a <u>bedroom</u>.
Compound word: bed + room

bees   (bēz) *n.* plural of *bee;* insects that feed on pollen
It takes many <u>bees</u> to make honey.

before   (bĭ fôr′) *prep.* in front of
Come in the house <u>before</u> it begins to rain.

began   (bĭ gan′) *v.* past tense of *begin*
It <u>began</u> to snow in the middle of the night.

believe   (bĭ lēv′) *v.* to accept something as real
We <u>believe</u> in the mercy of God.

bell   (bĕl) *n.* a hollow piece of metal that
makes a ringing sound when struck
The church <u>bell</u> rang for the service to begin.

below   (bĭ lō′) *adv.* in a lower place
John dove <u>below</u> the surface of the water.

belt   (bĕlt) *n.* a piece of leather or cloth used around the
waist to hold up trousers or shorts
Mother got John a new <u>belt</u>.

beside   (bĭ sīd′) *prep.* next to
Put the blue book <u>beside</u> the red one.

best   (bĕst) *adj.* the highest quality
Scott wore his <u>best</u> shirt and tie to church.
good, better, best

better   (bĕt′ ər) *adj.* comparative form of *good*
The sick child felt <u>better</u> after she slept.

between   (bǐ twēn′) *prep.* in a space that separates two objects
Hang the picture <u>between</u> the two statues.

beyond   (bǐ yǒnd′) *prep.* farther than something else
The sun set <u>beyond</u> the horizon.

bigger   (bǐg′ ər) *adj.* comparative form of *big*
Mark's sandwich was <u>bigger</u> than Jim's.

biggest   (bǐg′ əst) *adj.* superlative form of *big;* the largest
of all other things
That was the <u>biggest</u> cat I have ever seen!
big, bigger, biggest

bind   (bīnd) *v.* to tie, wrap, or fasten together
Ben needed to <u>bind</u> the dog's sore leg.
bind, binds, binding, bound

bitter   (bǐt′ ər) *adj.* unpleasant taste; sadness
That medicine was very <u>bitter</u>.

blame   (blām) *v.* accuse or find fault with
Don't <u>blame</u> John for the fall.
blame, blames, blaming, blamed

blend   (blĕnd) *v.* to mix together
Mom will help me <u>blend</u> the sugar,
eggs, and butter.
blend, blends, blending, blended

blow
(blō) *n.* to be hit by something
Jack suffered a <u>blow</u> to the head.
v. to move or to make a sound with air
The wind began to <u>blow</u> very hard.
blow, blows, blowing, blew

bluff
(blŭf) *n.* a cliff
Sarah likes to climb the <u>bluff</u>.
v. to fool
Beth tried to <u>bluff</u> her way out of trouble.
bluff, bluffs, bluffing, bluffed

bone
(bōn) *n.* part of a skeleton
Sam's dog likes to chew on a <u>bone</u>.

books
(bŭks) *n.* plural of *book*
Joe got three <u>books</u> at the library.

boot
(büt) *n.* a foot covering
Adam got one <u>boot</u> stuck in the mud.

both
(bōth) *adj.* two
Max and Carl will <u>both</u> go to
the game.

bottle
(bŏt′ əl) *n.* a container with a narrow top that usually
holds liquids
Wendy had a beautiful <u>bottle</u> from her grandmother.

boy's
(boiz) *n.* possessive of *boy;* belonging to the boy
The <u>boy's</u> car was red.

brave (brāv) *adj.* showing courage
Martin was very <u>brave</u> when he saved the little girl.

break (brāk) *n.* to take time off
We took a <u>break</u> from our work.
v. to shatter or smash something to pieces
Be careful not to <u>break</u> the china doll.
break, breaks, breaking, broke, broken

breakfast (brĕk′ f ə st) *n.* first meal of the day
David likes bacon and toast for <u>breakfast</u>.

bubble (bŭb′ əl) *n.* a thin, air-filled pocket of liquid
Jessie blew a gigantic soap <u>bubble</u>.

butter (bŭt′ ər) *n.* fatty substance made from cream, used
for spreading or cooking
Nathan likes <u>butter</u> and syrup on his pancakes.

by (bī) *prep.* (1) near; (2) along; (3) through effort
1. Please set the box <u>by</u> the table.
2. The stream ran <u>by</u> the old path.
3. The hard work was completed <u>by</u> Jim.

C

cage   (kāj) *n.* enclosure with a door used to confine something
The bird in the <u>cage</u> began to sing.

called   (kôld) *v.* past tense of *call*
Jeff <u>called</u> Jim on the phone.

cape   (kāp) *n.* loose outer garment
Kevin had a blue <u>cape</u> as part of his costume.

cattle   (kăt′ əl) *n.* animals, like cows, raised for meat or dairy products
Have you ever seen a <u>cattle</u> round-up?

center   (sĕn′ tər) *n.* a point in the middle
Tom stood in the <u>center</u> of the circle.

chick   (chĭk) *n.* baby chicken
The little yellow <u>chick</u> stayed close to its mother.

child's   (chīldz) *n.* possessive; belonging to the child
The <u>child's</u> book was on the table.

children's   (chĭl′ drənz) *n.* possessive; belonging to the children
The <u>children's</u> clothes were in the laundry.

chill	(chĭl) *n.* cold feeling
	Bill felt a <u>chill</u> when the cold wind blew.
	v. to cool down
	Please <u>chill</u> the water before serving it.
	chill, chills, chilling, chilled
chime	(chīm) *n.* a bell, or other metal piece which produces a sound when struck
	The <u>chime</u> on the clock struck ten.
	v. to ring a tone
	Did you hear the clock <u>chime</u>?
	chime, chimes, chiming, chimed
Christian	(krĭs' chən) *n.* a follower of Jesus Christ
	Steve is proud to be a <u>Christian</u>.
churches	(chėrch' əz) *n.* plural of *church*
	We visited two <u>churches</u> on our vacation.
circle	(sėrk' əl) *n.* round; a line that curves around to meet with each point the same distance from the center
	Join hands and make a <u>circle</u> around the room.
	v. to go around in a circle
	The runner will <u>circle</u> the track in a victory lap.
	circle, circles, circling, circled
circus	(sėr' kəs) *n.* traveling show with many acts
	We go to the <u>circus</u> every year.
	plural: circuses

11

clang   (klăng) *n.* a loud, ringing sound
The bell on the trolley went <u>clang</u>.
v. to make a loud, ringing sound
Did you hear the trolley bell <u>clang</u>?
clang, clangs, clanging, clanged

clasp   (klăsp) *n.* a fastener
Can you fix the <u>clasp</u> on my watch?
v. to hold together
Mother told Julie to <u>clasp</u> her hand tightly.
clasp, clasps, clasping, clasped

clay   (klā) *n.* a sticky, stiff type of earth that becomes hard
when it is baked.
Bill likes to make things out of <u>clay</u>.

class   (klăs) *n.* a group of students studying the same subject
Mrs. Johnson's <u>class</u> will go to the museum.
plural: classes

click   (klĭk) *n.* a sharp sound like a snapping noise
The <u>click</u> of the lock made Pat jump.
v. to make or cause a sharp, snapping noise
As he turned the key, Joe heard the lock <u>click</u>.
click, clicks, clicking, clicked

clothes   (klōz) *n.* articles of clothing: shirts,
dresses, slacks, etc.
What <u>clothes</u> will you pack
for camping?

cloud (kloud) *n.* ice or tiny water drops joined together in a mass that floats in the sky
A great white <u>cloud</u> passed over the house.
v. to cover or make something dark
Soap tends to <u>cloud</u> the water.
cloud, clouds, clouding, clouded

clown (kloun) *n.* a person who likes playing jokes; a circus performer who does tricks and wears funny makeup
Who is your favorite <u>clown</u> in the circus?
v. to play jokes on people or act funny
Bob likes to <u>clown</u> around with the little children.
clown, clowns, clowning, clowned

cob (kŏb) *n.* corncob
Grandma takes the corn off the <u>cob</u> before she cooks it.

cook (kŭk) *n.* a person who prepares food
Mark is a <u>cook</u> at the hotel dining room.
v. to prepare food
Peter learned to <u>cook</u> macaroni and cheese.
cook, cooks, cooking, cooked

cooked (kŭkt) *v.* past tense of *cook*
Mrs. White <u>cooked</u> dinner for ten people.

cool (kül) *adj.* not warm, not very cold
At sundown, a <u>cool</u> breeze began to blow.
cool, cooler, coolest
v. to make cool
Did you let the pie <u>cool</u> before you cut it?
cool, cools, cooling, cooled

cooled (küld) *v.* past tense of *cool*
The cookies must be <u>cooled</u> before you eat them.

cot (kŏt) *n.* a small bed that folds up
Mike slept on a <u>cot</u> in the tent.

couldn't (küd' nt) *contraction.* could not
Because it rained, we <u>couldn't</u> have a picnic.

count (kount) *v.* to recite numbers in a row
Jason could <u>count</u> from 1 to 1,000.
count, counts, counting, counted

cross (krŏs) *n.* an upright stick or wood beam
with a crossbar
Jesus died on a <u>cross</u> to save us.
plural: crosses
v. to lay something across, to
walk from one side to the other
Look both ways before you <u>cross</u> the street.
cross, crosses, crossing, crossed

14

cry
(krī) *n.* a shout or loud noise
We heard an animal's <u>cry</u> in the forest
plural: cries
v. sobbing or shedding tears
The baby began to <u>cry</u> because he
was afraid.
cry, cries, crying, cried

cuff
(kŭf) *n.* a fold or band at the end of a sleeve
or trouser leg
Andy got ice cream on the <u>cuff</u> of his shirt sleeve.

curb
(kėrb) *n.* a raised step at the street edge
of a sidewalk
Stay on the <u>curb</u> until the light changes.

cut
(kŭt) *n.* a wound or opening made by a sharp object
Bill had a <u>cut</u> on his finger.
v. to make a slice or opening in something.
Jenny <u>cut</u> the apple into four pieces.
cut, cuts, cutting, cut

D

daddy   (dăd′ ē) *n.* father
Daddy and Bill will go to the park.

day   (dā) *n.* one 24-hour space of time
Today was a very sunny, warm day.

dear   (dĭr) *adj.* much loved and cared about
The small doll was very dear to Sarah.

December   (dĭ sem′ b ə r) *n.* the 12th month
of the year
We celebrate Christmas in December.

deer   (dĭr) *n.* a four-legged animal that can run swiftly;
a cud-chewing animal
We saw two deer in the meadow.

didn't   (dĭd′ nt) *contraction.* did not
Nancy didn't have time to go to the fair.

dinner   (dĭn′ ə r) *n.* the main meal of the day
Mother invited the neighbors for dinner.

dirt   (dėrt) *n.* soil, earth, ground
Kelly loved to play in the dirt.

dock
(dŏk) *n.* pier; a long surface built out from the shore over the water where ships/boats are tied down
The ship moved away from the <u>dock</u>.
v. to secure a boat or ship
The ocean liner will <u>dock</u> at Pier 19.
dock, docks, docking, docked

dream
(drēm) *n.* a hope for the future; thoughts or feelings that pass through the mind as we sleep
Julie's <u>dream</u> is to be a nurse when she grows up.
v. to have hopes or dreams
Ben likes to <u>dream</u> about owning a big house someday.
dream, dreams, dreaming, dreamed

duck
(dŭk) *n.* a bird with short legs and webbed feet that swims
The little <u>duck</u> was learning to swim.
v. to lower your head or your body to avoid hitting something or being hit by something
We had to <u>duck</u> quickly when the ball whizzed by our heads.
duck, ducks, ducking, ducked

E

each   (ēch) *adj.* referring to one or more persons or things individually
The teacher stopped to help <u>each</u> child.

early   (ėr´ lē) *adv.* near the start of something
We have to get up very <u>early</u> tomorrow.

earth   (ėrth) *n.* the world, the planet on which we live
God made the heavens and the <u>earth</u>.

eighteen   (ā´ tēn´) *n.* the number between 17 and 19
Bob's brother, Jim, will be <u>eighteen</u> in June.

eighth   (ātth) *adj.* thing coming after the 7th in a series
Sally will be in the <u>eighth</u> grade next year.

eighty   (ā´ tē) *n.* number eight times ten
Jake's grandma just turned <u>eighty</u>.

elephant   (ĕl´ ə fənt) *n.* a very large animal with thick, gray skin, tusks, and a long trunk
That <u>elephant</u> has very long tusks.

eleven   (ĭ lĕv′ ən) *n.* number between
10 and 12
The plane arrives at <u>eleven</u> o'clock
this morning.

enclose   (ĕn klōz′) *v.* to surround something or shut it in
Dad will <u>enclose</u> the yard with a fence.
enclose, encloses, enclosing, enclosed

enjoy   (ĕn joi′) *v.* to take pleasure in, to receive joy from
Did you <u>enjoy</u> the puppet show?
enjoy, enjoys, enjoying, enjoyed

enjoyment   (ĕn joi′ mĕnt) *n.* joy
The children's <u>enjoyment</u> was seen on their faces.

enlarge   (ĕn lärj′) *v.* to make bigger
Mary will <u>enlarge</u> the photo.
enlarge, enlarges, enlarging, enlarged

entire   (ĕn tīr′) *adj.* all; including everything or everyone
Mr. Bell's <u>entire</u> class will go to the game.

entrust   (ĕn trŭst′) *v.* to give the care of
something or someone to another
I will <u>entrust</u> my pet to you while
I'm gone.
entrust, entrusts, entrusting, entrusted

19

F

fearless (fĭr′ lĭs) *adj.* brave
John was <u>fearless</u> in the face of danger.

February (fĕb′ rü er′ ē) *n.* the 2nd month of the year
Valentine's Day is <u>February</u> 14th.

fifteen (fĭf tēn′) n. a number between 14 and 16
Mary's brother will be <u>fifteen</u> in June.

fifth (fĭfth) *adj.* coming after the 4th in a series
Sam is going into the <u>fifth</u> grade.

fifty (fĭf′ tē) *n.* number five times ten
Dad will be <u>fifty</u> tomorrow.
adj. five times ten of something
Jill sold <u>fifty</u> boxes of cookies.

flake (flāk) *n.* small piece or chip of something
Have you ever looked closely at a <u>flake</u> of snow?

flame (flām) *n.* burning part of a fire
Turn up the <u>flame</u> under the soup.

flew (flü) *v.* past tense of *fly*
Six birds <u>flew</u> over our heads.

float (flōt) *v.* to rest on top of the water
Do you know how to <u>float</u>?
float, floats, floating, floated

flower   (flou′ ər) *n.* part of a plant that blooms and bears seeds
That red <u>flower</u> is very beautiful.

foam   (fōm) *n.* tiny bubbles that form on top of a liquid
The seagulls dive through the <u>foam</u> on the waves.

forgetful   (fər gĕt′ fəl) *adj.* having a hard time remembering things
Try not to be so <u>forgetful</u> about your homework.

forgot   (fər gŏt′) *v.* past tense of *forget*
I almost <u>forgot</u> to go to Jack's party.

forty   (fôr′ tē) *adj.* number ten times four
Jesus spent <u>forty</u> days in the desert.

found   (found) *v.* past tense of *find*; to recover something that was lost
Bob <u>found</u> three dollars on the ground.

fourteen   (fôr′ tēn′) *n.* a number between 13 and 15
Martha will be <u>fourteen</u> on her next birthday.

fourth   (fôrth) *adj.* coming after the 3rd in a series
Is Sam in the <u>fourth</u> grade?

fox   (fŏks) *n.* wild animal with a pointed nose and a bushy tail, usually with reddish-brown fur
A small <u>fox</u> ran across the trail.

foxes   (fŏks′ əz) *n.* plural of *fox*
We saw three <u>foxes</u> in their den.

foxhole   (fŏks′ hōl) *n.* a hole dug by soldiers as a hiding place
The soldiers had to practice digging a <u>foxhole</u>.

Friday   (frī′ dē) *n.* the 6th day of the week
We'll go to the baseball game on <u>Friday</u>.

friendship   (frĕnd′ ship) *n.* close feeling or
relationship between two people
A <u>friendship</u> is a very special thing.

fries   (frīz) *n.* the plural short form of *French fry*
The girls had hamburgers and <u>fries</u> for lunch.
v. present tense of *fry*
Mom <u>fries</u> fish for us on Fridays.
fry, fries, frying, fried

fur   (fėr) *n.* soft, often thick hair that covers many animals
The rabbit had soft, white <u>fur</u>.

G

gas
(găs) *n.* neither solid nor liquid; short form of *gasoline*
Our car nearly ran out of <u>gas</u>.

geese
(gēs) *n.* plural of *goose*
Did you see the <u>geese</u> flying south?

giant
(jī′ ənt) *n.* person or thing that is
very strong and very large
Tim looked like a <u>giant</u> next to his little brother.

giggle
(gĭg′ əl) *n.* a silly laugh
Beth's <u>giggle</u> makes other people laugh.
v. to laugh in a nervous way
Beth started to <u>giggle</u> and couldn't stop.
giggle, giggles, giggling, giggled

ginger
(jĭn′ jər) *n.* a spice that comes from the root of the
ginger plant
Mom puts <u>ginger</u> in her Chinese chicken.

girl's
(gĕrlz) *n.* possessive, belonging to the girl
The <u>girl's</u> hair was very curly.

glad
(glăd) *adj.* happy, feeling joy
We were <u>glad</u> to hear Jim was feeling better.

glasses   (glăs′ əz) *n.* plural of *glass*
Ken was thirsty, so he drank two <u>glasses</u> of water.

globe   (glōb) *n.* a round object; a small model of the earth
Please find Africa on the <u>globe</u>.

glue   (glü) *n.* a sticky substance used to
attach things together
Use <u>glue</u> when you make your model airplane.
v. to attach things together with a sticky substance
Please <u>glue</u> these broken pieces together.
glue, glues, gluing, glued

gnash   (năsh) *v.* to grind teeth together
Don't <u>gnash</u> your teeth.
gnash, gnashes, gnashing, gnashed

gnaw   (nô) *v.* to chew on, to wear down
Ben watched his dog <u>gnaw</u> on a bone.
gnaw, gnaws, gnawing, gnawed

gnome   (nōm) *n.* a dwarf in a fairy tale
A <u>gnome</u> is a very small creature.

goose   (güs) *n.* a bird that swims like a
duck but has a larger body and a longer neck
Mitch and Sue have a white <u>goose</u> for a pet.

gopher   (go' f ə r) *n.* a small, furry rodent with pockets
in its cheeks
A <u>gopher</u> has invaded our garden!

grade   (grād) *n.* a section or division of a
school; a mark for work in a course
Mitch will be in the second <u>grade</u> this year.
v. to give a mark or judgment on work performed
The teacher will <u>grade</u> our tests when we are done.
grade, grades, grading, graded

grateful   (grāt' f ə l) *adj.* thankful
I am very <u>grateful</u> to God for all He has given me.

grow   (grō) *v.* to get larger or taller
The corn in the field began to <u>grow</u> very tall.
grow, grows, growing, grew

guess   (gĕs) *v.* to judge something or make a decision
about it
Can you <u>guess</u> who will come to the party?
guess, guesses, guessing, guessed

gum   (gŭm) *n.* a sticky substance that trees and plants
produce; *chewing gum*
Please do not chew <u>gum</u> in school.

25

H

hammer

(hăm′ ər) *n.* a tool used for striking
nails or breaking things
Please bring me the <u>hammer</u> and some nails.

handful

(hănd′ fŭl) *n.* as much of a thing as one hand can
hold
Bill grabbed a <u>handful</u> of chips.

hands

(hăndz) *n.* plural of *hand*
Did you wash your <u>hands</u> before supper?

hang

(hăng) *v.* to fasten or hook something to a line
or platform
Will you <u>hang</u> the clothes on the line to dry?
hang, hangs, hanging, hung

happier

(hăp′ ē ər) *adj.* comparative of *happy*
I have never seen Judy <u>happier</u>
than she is now.

happiest

(hăp′ ē əst) *adj.* superlative of *happy*; most happy
This was the <u>happiest</u> birthday I have ever had!

headache

(hĕd′ āk) *n.* a pain in one's head
The loud noise gave Mom a <u>headache</u>.

hear

(hĭr) *v.* to receive sound and interpret it
Did you <u>hear</u> that new song on the radio?

he'd   (hēd) *contraction.* he had, he would
Kevin said that <u>he'd</u> be here before noon.

he'll   (hēl) *contraction.* he will
He said that <u>he'll</u> bring the lunch.

helpful   (hĕlp' f ə l) *adj.* giving help; being of use
When we were moving, Martha was very <u>helpful</u>.

helpless   (hĕlp' lĕs) *adj.* unable to care for oneself
The hurt puppy was very <u>helpless</u>.

hem   (hĕm) *n.* the finished edge of a piece of cloth
The <u>hem</u> came out of her skirt.
v. to fold the raw edge of a piece of cloth and sew it
Mother will <u>hem</u> the skirt for me.
hem, hems, hemming, hemmed

here   (hĭr) *adv.* being at a place
Please come <u>here</u> and help me.

hers   (hėrz) *pronoun.* possessive of *her*
Rhonda said that the book was <u>hers</u>.

hiked   (hīkt) *v.* past tense of *hike*
Greg and Tom <u>hiked</u> into the canyon.

him   (hĭm) *pronoun.* form of *he*
Ted asked Jenna to help <u>him</u>.

hood   (hụd) *n.* a covering for the head,
often attached to a jacket
You'll need to use your <u>hood</u> in this wind.

hopeless   (hōp′ lĭs) *adj.* discouraged; without hope
When all seems <u>hopeless</u>, God is still there.

hot   (hŏt) *adj.* high temperature
This summer will be very <u>hot</u>.

hour   (our) *n.* 60 minutes
I'll meet you in an <u>hour</u>.

houses   (hou′ s ə z) *n.* plural of *house*
All of the <u>houses</u> on our street look the same.

how   (hou) *adv.* in what way a thing is done
Show John <u>how</u> to address the letter.

huddle   (hŭd′ d ə l) *n.* things or people crowded together
The football team was in a <u>huddle</u>.

huge   (hyüj) *adj.* very large
Did you see that <u>huge</u> elephant?

hundred   (hŭn′ dr ə d) *adj.* being ten times ten
Bill gave one <u>hundred</u> dollars to help the poor.

I

ice (īs) *n.* frozen water
Pick up some <u>ice</u> for the picnic, please.

I'd (īd) *contraction.* I had, I would
Sally thought that <u>I'd</u> be going with her.

inside (in sīd') *n.* the part that is within
Go <u>inside</u> and warm up.

its (its) *pronoun.* possessive of *it*
The kitten was napping in <u>its</u> bed.

it's (its) *contraction.* it is
Mary says that <u>it's</u> time to leave for church.

29

J

January (jăn′ yü er′ ē) *n.* the 1st month of the year
January 1st is New Year's Day.

joke (jōk) *n.* a trick or a funny story
Benny's joke was very funny.

judgment (jŭj′ m ə nt) *n.* a decision about something important
You use good judgment when you obey your parents.

juggle (jŭg′ əl) *v.* skill of doing many things with the hands
or tossing many things at one time
The clown can juggle four balls
at one time.
juggle, juggles, juggling, juggled

July (jù lī′) *n.* the 7th month of the year
My birthday is in July.

June (jün) *n.* the 6th month of the year
Elizabeth will be five years old in June.

K

kettle   (kĕt′ əl) *n.* a pot used to boil water or other liquids
Put the tea <u>kettle</u> on to boil, please.

kites   (kīts) *n.* plural of *kite*
We went to the park to fly our <u>kites</u>.

kneads   (nēdz) *v.* present tense of *knead*; to press or mix
dough together with the hands
When Mom <u>kneads</u> the bread, I like to watch.

knee   (nē) *n.* the joint between the lower
and upper part of the leg
Al fell and skinned his <u>knee</u>.

knees   (nēz) *n.* plural of *knee*
You need to protect your <u>knees</u> when skating.

kneel   (nēl) *v.* to rest on the knees
I <u>kneel</u> beside my bed each night to say my prayers.
kneel, kneels, kneeling, knelt

knife   (nīf) *n.* a flat, sharp blade used for slicing or cutting
Be very careful with that sharp <u>knife</u>!

knight   (nīt) *n.* a man of honor in the Middle Ages
The <u>knight</u> sat very tall on his horse.

knives   (nīvz) *n.* plural of *knife*
Please put the forks, spoons, and <u>knives</u> on the table.

known   (nōn) *v.* past participle of *know*
How long have you <u>known</u> Zack?

knows   (nōz) *v.* present tense of *know*
Sue <u>knows</u> the way to the park.

L

ladder (lăd′ ər) *n.* a frame or device with rungs, used to climb to high places
We'll need a <u>ladder</u> to reach the roof.

learn (lėrn) *v.* to come to know something
We often <u>learn</u> by watching others.
learn, learns, learning, learned

leg (lĕg) *n.* a part of the body used for walking or standing
Jim had his <u>leg</u> in a cast.

lemon (lĕm′ ən) *n.* a small, yellow citrus fruit with a sour taste
Ivan likes <u>lemon</u> in his iced tea.

letter (lĕt′ ər) *n.* a written message sent to someone; a single figure in an alphabet
I received a <u>letter</u> from my brother.

lick (lĭk) *v.* to rub the tongue across something
Hurry up and <u>lick</u> that ice cream cone before it melts!
lick, licks, licking, licked

life (līf) *n.* being alive, the span of one's time on earth
Put your <u>life</u> in God's hands.

lip   (lĭp) *n.* the upper and lower outside edges of the mouth
When Nancy fell, she cut her <u>lip</u>.

littler   (lĭtl′ ər) *adj.* comparative of *little*
The white kitten was <u>littler</u> than the black one.

littlest   (lĭtl′ əst) *adj.* superlative of *little*
The black puppy was the <u>littlest</u> of all the puppies.

lives   (līvz) *n.* plural of *life*
Our <u>lives</u> belong to God.
(lĭvz) *v.* present tense of *live*
Jack <u>lives</u> just around the corner from me.
live, lives, living, lived

loaded   (lōd′ əd) *v.* past tense of *load*
We <u>loaded</u> the cart with groceries.

looked   (lŭkt) *v.* past tense of *look*
Jim <u>looked</u> for an hour before he found his keys.

low   (lō) *adj.* not high
Dad has a very <u>low</u> voice.

luck   (lŭk) *n.* good fortune
Bob had no <u>luck</u> finding his lost jacket.

lung   (lŭng) *n.* one of two organs in the chest used in breathing
She had an infection in her right <u>lung</u>.

M

map   (măp) *n.* a drawing that shows
where something is located
Can you find our street on the <u>map</u>?

March   (märch) *n.* the 3rd month of the year
Joe is coming to visit in <u>March</u>.

math   (măth) *n.* study of numbers, short for *mathematics*
Betty's favorite subject is <u>math</u>.

May   (mā) *n.* the 5th month of the year
Our school ends in <u>May</u>.

meatloaf   (mēt′ lōf) *n.* a main dish made of meat and
vegetables and baked in the form of a loaf
Victor likes <u>meatloaf</u> sandwiches.
Compound word: meat + loaf

meek   (mēk) *adj.* patient, humble, mild
Jesus is <u>meek</u> and humble of heart.

melted   (mĕlt′ əd) *v.* past tense of *melt*
The ice cream <u>melted</u> quickly in the sun.

men   (mĕn) *n.* plural of *man*
How many <u>men</u> do we need for the job?

met   (mĕt) *v.* past tense of *meet*
Tom <u>met</u> Will at the park.

35

mice (mīs) *n.* plural of *mouse*
We saw four <u>mice</u> race across the field.

middle (mĭd′ əl) *n.* point halfway between two other points
Put the vase of flowers on the <u>middle</u> of the shelf.

mix (mĭks) *v.* to stir or blend together
I like to help Mom <u>mix</u> the cookie dough.

mixed (mĭkst) *v.* past tense of *mix*
Mom and I <u>mixed</u> the cookie dough.

mixes (mĭks′ əz) *v.* present tense of *mix*
Mom <u>mixes</u> the cookie dough while I help.

mommy (mŏm′ ē) *n.* mother
Her <u>mommy</u> gave her a ride in the stroller.

Monday (mŭn′ dē) *n.* the 2nd day of the week
Next <u>Monday</u> we will go to the zoo.

moonlight (mün′ līt) *n.* rays of light shining from the moon
The <u>moonlight</u> came in the bedroom window.
Compound word: moon + light

mop

(mŏp) *n.* cloth or sponge at the
end of a handle used to dust or wash
the floor
We need to buy a new <u>mop</u> for the
kitchen.
v. to wash, wipe, or dry
Please <u>mop</u> the floors before you leave.
mop, mops, mopping, mopped

morning

(môrn′ ing) *n.* the part of the day
before noon
What time did you wake up this <u>morning</u>?

mouth

(mouth) *n.* the part of the body which takes in food
and produces sounds
He always talks with his <u>mouth</u> full of food.

must

(mŭst) *v.* to have to do something
I <u>must</u> remember to bring the books to the library.
must, must, must

N

needs   (nēdz) *v.* present tense of *need*
            Jim's sister <u>needs</u> some new clothes.

nerve   (nėrv) *n.* a part of the body's message system
            She damaged a <u>nerve</u> in her finger.

new   (nü) *adj.* not used
            Our family just bought a <u>new</u> house.

nibble   (nĭb′ əl) *v.* to eat with quick, tiny bites
            I watched a mouse <u>nibble</u> on some cheese.
            nibble, nibbles, nibbling, nibbled

nineteen   (nīn′ tēn′) *n.* a number between 18 and 20
            Al will be <u>nineteen</u> on Friday.

ninety   (nīn′ tē) *n.* being ten times nine
            Jake's grandpa is <u>ninety</u> years old.

ninth   (nīnth) *adj.* next in a series after the 8th
            She was the <u>ninth</u> person to arrive.

no   (nō) *adj.* not any
            We have <u>no</u> pancakes left.

nod   (nŏd) *v.* to move the head forward in agreement;
            to let the head drop forward when falling asleep
            The girl began to <u>nod</u> off to sleep.
            nod, nods, nodding, nodded

noon (nün) *n.* middle of the day; 12 o'clock in the daytime
Meet me at <u>noon</u> on Sunday.

nose (nōz) *n.* the opening in the face above the mouth
used for breathing and smelling
My <u>nose</u> itches.

November (nō věm′ bər) *n.* the 11th month of the year
Thanksgiving Day is in <u>November</u>.

nowhere (nō′ hwer) *adv.* not any place
We had <u>nowhere</u> to go this weekend.
Compound word: no + where

O

October (ŏk tō′ b ə r) *n.* the 10th month of the year
The leaves turn color in <u>October</u>.

off (ŏf) *adv.* to move away from
He took <u>off</u> his hat in the house.

outside (out sīd′) *n.* side of something that faces out
It was rainy <u>outside</u> this morning.

ox (ŏks) *n.* a large animal that chews a cud
and is used on a farm
The <u>ox</u> was pulling the cart.

oxen (ŏks′ ə n) *n.* plural of *ox*
A team of <u>oxen</u> were pulling a plow.

P

paddle (păd′ əl) *n.* a stick used to row a boat
The <u>paddle</u> for this canoe is very heavy.
v. to row or move a boat along
Can you help <u>paddle</u> the canoe?
paddle, paddles, paddling, paddled

page (pāj) *n.* one side of a paper in a book or magazine
On what <u>page</u> does the story begin?

patchwork (păch′ wėrk) *adj.* a pattern or design made from
sewing pieces of cloth together
Grandma made a <u>patchwork</u> quilt for my birthday.
Compound word: patch + work

path (păth) *n.* a way or track that
leads to something
The <u>path</u> led into a beautiful garden.

peaches (pēch′ əz) *n.* plural of *peach*
We went to the orchard to pick <u>peaches</u>.

pencil (pĕn′ s əl) *n.* a long, thin tool for writing made
of wood and a writing substance such as graphite
You'll need a sharp <u>pencil</u> for the test.

pet   (pĕt) *n.* a tame animal kept by a person or family
What kind of <u>pet</u> do you have?
v. to pat gently
May I <u>pet</u> the cat?
pet, pets, petting, petted

pets   (pĕts) *n.* plural of *pet*
Mark has four different <u>pets</u>.

phonics   (fŏn′ ĭks) *n.* sounds of different letters and groups
of letters
You will study <u>phonics</u> this year.

photograph   (fō′ tə graf) *n.* a picture taken by a camera
Here is a <u>photograph</u> of my great-grandmother.

pick   (pĭk) *v.* to choose something; to gather something up
Please <u>pick</u> up that spoon off the floor.
pick, picks, picking, picked

pine   (pīn) *n.* an evergreen tree with needles and
seed cones
We have a very tall <u>pine</u> tree in our front yard.

pizza   (pēt′ sə) *n.* an Italian "pie" made of bread dough with
tomatoes, cheese, and other ingredients
Mom ordered <u>pizza</u> for supper as a treat.

plan (plăn) *n.* an idea or map of how something will be done
What plan do you have for the picnic?
v. to make a way of doing something
I plan to go to the park.
plan, plans, planning, planned

plate (plāt) *n.* a dish, usually round and shallow, used for serving and eating food
Wash your plate when you finish eating.

played (plād) *v.* past tense of play
Martin and Joe played with each other.

please (plez) *v.* to give someone pleasure
It would please me if you would do your homework.
please, pleases, pleasing, pleased

plow (plou) *n.* a farm tool for cutting soil and preparing fields for planting
Did you see that old plow in the museum?
v. to turn the ground for planting
Bob likes to help his father plow the field.
plow, plows, plowing, plowed

poke (pōk) *n.* a jab given by a finger or a stick
He gave Bill a poke to wake him up.
v. to jab something or someone with a finger or a stick
Don't poke John when he is studying.
poke, pokes, poking, poked

pond　　　　(pŏnd) *n.* a small lake or body of water
We went to the <u>pond</u> to go swimming.

pool　　　　(pül) *n.* a small body of water used for swimming
It's nice to have a <u>pool</u> in the summer.

praise　　　　(prāz) *n.* words or songs that show good will toward
someone
Sing <u>praise</u> to God!
v. to say good things about someone or something
We will <u>praise</u> the Lord in all we do.
praise, praises, praising, praised

prayed　　　　(prād) *v.* past tense of *pray*
Our church <u>prayed</u> for the sick man.

prettiest　　　　(prĭt′ ē əst) *adj.* superlative of *pretty*
The red rose is the <u>prettiest</u> flower in the bouquet.

puddle　　　　(pŭd′ əl) *n.* a small pool of water,
or water and mud, left after a
rainfall or watering
Beth jumped in the <u>puddle</u>.

puppies　　　　(pŭp′ ēz) *n.* plural of *puppy*
The dog had six <u>puppies</u>.

purse   (pėrs) *n.* a small bag or container for carrying money
and other items
Molly had a new blue <u>purse</u>.

puzzle   (pŭz′ əl) *n.* a question or problem that needs
to be solved
Nate worked on a crossword <u>puzzle</u>.

Q

quest   (kwĕst) *n.* a journey or adventure
The knight went on a <u>quest</u> for glory.

quiet   (kwī′ ət) *adj.* without noise
Please be <u>quiet</u> while Mom takes
a nap.

quietly   (kwī′ ə t lē) *adv.* without noise
Please walk <u>quietly</u> when the baby is asleep.

quilt   (kwĭlt) *n.* a kind of blanket made from squares
and layers of cloth sewn together
Grandma made me a <u>quilt</u> for my birthday.

quiz   (kwĭz) *n.* a short test
We'll have a spelling <u>quiz</u> on Wednesday.

R

rabbit (răb′ ĭt) *n.* a small animal that burrows, has soft fur, long ears, and a short tail
Erin showed a gray <u>rabbit</u> in the pet show.

rang (răng) *v.* past tense of *ring*
When the bell <u>rang</u>, the children came in.

rattle (răt′ əl) *n.* a toy filled with a material to make a sharp sound when shaken
The baby dropped her <u>rattle</u>.
v. to make a sharp, repeated sound
Did you hear the windows <u>rattle</u> in the wind?
rattle, rattles, rattling, rattled

read (rēd) *v.* to speak or get the meaning of written words
Please <u>read</u> me a story.
(rĕd) *v.* past tense of *read*
I <u>read</u> a story last night.
read, reads, reading, read

reed (rēd) *n.* a tall grass; a thin piece of wood used in musical instruments
John used a <u>reed</u> to make a flute.

rich (rich) *adj.* wealthy; having much money
A person who has good friends is <u>rich</u>.

riddle   (rĭd′ əl) *n.* a mystery or written question to solve
Can you solve this <u>riddle</u>?

ring   (rĭng) *n.* a thin band of metal worn on the finger
Dad gave Mom a <u>ring</u> for their anniversary.
v. to make a sound, like a bell
Did you hear the phone <u>ring</u>?
ring, rings, ringing, rang, rung

rock   (rŏk) *n.* a piece of stone
Bob has a large <u>rock</u> in his collection.
v. to move back and forth
Mother will <u>rock</u> the baby to sleep.
rock, rocks, rocking, rocked

roof   (rüf) *n.* the top covering of a building or house
After the storm, our <u>roof</u> began to leak.

rope   (rōp) *n.* a thick, strong cord
Becky used a strong <u>rope</u> as a leash for her dog.
v. to fasten something with a rope
John likes to <u>rope</u> steers.
rope, ropes, roping, roped

roughly   (rŭf′ lē) *adv.* to share or handle without being careful
The child handled the puppy <u>roughly</u>.

row   (rō) *n.* things or people placed in a line
We sat in the third <u>row</u> in the
auditorium.
v. to move a boat across water
using oars
Can you <u>row</u> a boat?
row, rows, rowing, rowed

rubber   (rŭb′ ə r) *n.* a substance used
to make tires, boots, etc.
I have rain boots made of <u>rubber</u>.

rung   (rŭng) *n.* a step on a ladder
She stood on the third <u>rung</u> of the ladder.
v. past participle of *ring*
The cell phone has <u>rung</u> six times.

S

sack
(săk) *n.* a bag used to carry things
Ned carried his lunch in a paper <u>sack</u>.

saddle
(săd′ əl) *n.* a seat of a bicycle or a seat put
on a horse for riding
Matt has a new <u>saddle</u> for his horse.
v. to put a seat on a horse
Anna knows how to <u>saddle</u> her horse.
saddle, saddles, saddling, saddled

sang
(săng) *v.* past tense of *sing*
The choir <u>sang</u> many new hymns.

sat
(săt) *v.* past tense of *sit*
Mark <u>sat</u> on the chair next to me.

Saturday
(săt′ ər dā) *n.* the 7th day of the week
Last <u>Saturday</u> we went to the fair.

scarf
(skärf) *n.* a long piece of material usually used to wrap
around the head or neck
Mom has a new blue <u>scarf</u>.

scarves
(skärvz) *n.* plural of scarf
Jessica has many colorful <u>scarves</u>.

scene   (sēn) *n.* a place where something
happens; a part of a play or movie
The last <u>scene</u> in the play was funny.

scent   (sĕnt) *n.* an odor or smell
The flower has a lovely <u>scent</u>.

science   (sī´ əns) *n.* the study of the nature of things in the
world
Lynn just finished her <u>science</u> project.

scissors   (sĭz´ ərz) n. a tool used for cutting
May I please borrow your <u>scissors</u>?

scribble   (skrĭb´ əl) *v.* to make marks that have no meaning
Paul likes to <u>scribble</u> on scratch paper.
scribble, scribbles, scribbling, scribbled

script   (skrĭpt) *n.* the outline of a story and the characters'
words for a play
We worked on the <u>script</u> for the class play.

scrub   (skrŭb) *v.* to wash something by rubbing very hard
Pam needs to help Mom <u>scrub</u> the floor.
scrub, scrubs, scrubbing, scrubbed

second   (sĕk´ ənd) *adj.* next in a series after the first
Our team came in <u>second</u> place in the race.
n. one part of a minute
Please give me a <u>second</u> to finish this work.

seek (sēk) *v.* to look for
If we <u>seek</u> Jesus, we will find Him.
seek, seeks, seeking, sought

seen (sēn) *v.* past participle of *see*
Has anyone <u>seen</u> Paul's lost toy?

September (sĕp tem′ bər) *n.* the 9th month of the year
School begins again in <u>September</u> for many of us.

seventeen (sĕv′ ən tēn) *adj.* being one more than sixteen
I counted <u>seventeen</u> ducks in the pond.

seventh (sĕv′ ənth) *adj.* next in order after the 6th
James was <u>seventh</u> in line for lunch.

seventy (sĕv′ ən tē) *n.* the number ten times seven
Jesus says we must forgive <u>seventy</u> times seven.

sheep (shēp) *n.* a wool-covered animal related to a goat
We have seven <u>sheep</u> on
our farm.
plural: sheep

she's (shēz) *contraction.* she is, she has
<u>She's</u> going to the park with us.

shine (shīn) *v.* (1) to give off light (2) to polish
1. Let your light <u>shine</u> before all.
2. I can <u>shine</u> my shoes all by myself.
shine, shines, shining, shone

shoeless (shü′ ləs) *adj.* having no shoes
The <u>shoeless</u> child looked very sad.

shook (shük) *v.* past tense of *shake*
The two men <u>shook</u> hands when they met.

shouldn't (shüd′ nt) *contraction.* should not
We <u>shouldn't</u> ever lie to get out of trouble.

shout (shout) *n.* a loud cry
Jim's <u>shout</u> was heard in the next room.
v. to yell or cry out
Some Psalms tell us to <u>shout</u> with joy!
shout, shouts, shouting, shouted

sick (sĭk) *adj.* not well; ill
Sue was <u>sick</u> with the chicken pox.

sight (sīt) *n.* something that can be seen
The sunset was a beautiful <u>sight</u>.

sing (sĭng) *v.* to make musical sounds with the voice
We should <u>sing</u> a new song to the Lord!
sing, sings, singing, sang, sung

sip (sĭp) *n.* a small portion of liquid
Donald took a <u>sip</u> of the hot soup.
v. to take a small portion of liquid
I like to <u>sip</u> my lemonade through a straw.
sip, sips, sipping, sipped

sir (sėr) *n.* a word or title used to show respect to a man
The letter began, "Dear <u>Sir</u>."

sixteen (sĭks tēn´) *adj.* being one more than fifteen
Our class had <u>sixteen</u> children in it.

sixth (sĭks th) *adj.* next in a series after the 5th
The <u>sixth</u> grade class helped with the picnic.

sixty (sĭks´ tē) *adj.* being ten times six
Xavier needed <u>sixty</u> cents more to buy the ticket.

skate (skāt) *n.* a short form of *ice skate* or *roller skate*
The <u>skate</u> was ready to put on.
v. to roll or move along on skates
Can you roller <u>skate</u>?
skate, skates, skating, skated

slow (slō) *adj.* not fast-moving or quick
The car in front of us was very <u>slow</u>.

smaller (smôl´ ər) *adj.* comparative of *small*
Penny is <u>smaller</u> than Marcy.

smallest (smôl´ ə st) *adj.* superlative of *small*
The mustard seed is one of the <u>smallest</u> seeds.

smart (smärt) *adj.* wise or intelligent
It's <u>smart</u> to bring your umbrella on a rainy day.

smile
(smīl) *n.* a facial expression showing happiness
Justin has a very nice <u>smile</u>.
v. to show a smile, to be happy
Greg's humor made us all <u>smile</u>.
smile, smiles, smiling, smiled

snack
(snăk) *n.* a light meal
We brought apples for a <u>snack</u>.
v. to eat a light meal
Alex likes to <u>snack</u> on fries.
snack, snacks, snacking, snacked

snuggle
(snŭg' əl) v. to cuddle up close
Bonnie likes to <u>snuggle</u> in the blankets.
snuggle, snuggles, snuggling, snuggled

soap
(sōp) *n.* a powder, liquid, or solid substance used for washing
We need to buy more <u>soap</u> for the bathroom.

sock
(sŏk) *n.* a foot covering
John lost one <u>sock</u> in the gym.
v. to hit someone or something
It is not nice to <u>sock</u> anyone.

somehow
(sŭm hou) *adv.* in a way not yet known
We'll find another team member <u>somehow</u>.
Compound word: some + how

someone   (sŭm′ wŭn) *pronoun.* somebody
Will <u>someone</u> please help us out?
Compound word: some + one

song   (sŏng) *n.* sung music
The bird's <u>song</u> was very pretty.

south   (south) *n.* a direction opposite of north
The school is located on the <u>south</u> side of the street.

spell   (spĕl) *v.* to write out or say in order the letters that
make up a word
Can you <u>spell</u> that hard word?
spell, spells, spelling, spelled

splash   (splăsh) *n.* water or liquid sent through the air
John made a big <u>splash</u> when he jumped into the pool.
v. to make water or liquid scatter and fall
The kids liked to <u>splash</u> in the tub.
splash, splashes, splashing, splashed

spoon   (spün) *n.* a utensil used for stirring or eating food
or drinks
Will you please hand me a serving <u>spoon</u>?

spray   (sprā) *v.* to spread a liquid as a fine mist
We like to play in the <u>spray</u>
on a hot day.
spray, sprays, spraying, sprayed

56

squeak

(skwēk) *n.* a short, high−pitched sound
The dog's toy made a funny <u>squeak</u>.

stay

(stā) *v.* to remain
Please <u>stay</u> with us a little longer.
stay, stays, staying, stayed

stem

(stĕm) *n.* the main shoot of a plant or flower
The rose had a very long <u>stem</u>.

stir

(stėr) *v.* to mix
Will you please <u>stir</u> the soup for me?
stir, stirs, stirring, stirred

stood

(stŭd) *v.* past tense of *stand*
We <u>stood</u> by the bus stop
and waited.

stranger

(strān′ jər) *n.* someone who is unknown to us
The <u>stranger</u> asked the pastor for some help.

string

(strĭng) *n.* a thin cord or thread used for tying things
The cat likes to play with a ball of <u>string</u>.
v. to put things up in a line on a string
Will you help me <u>string</u> the Christmas lights?
string, strings, stringing, strung

stripe

(strīp) *n.* a line or band painted or sewn on something
Bill's shirt had a red <u>stripe</u> around the middle.

strong (strông) *adj.* powerful
The rope that held the boat in place was <u>strong</u>.

stronger (strông′ gər) *adj.* comparative of *strong*
Rope is <u>stronger</u> than string.

strongest (strông′ gəst) *adj.* superlative of *strong*
Greg is the <u>strongest</u> person I know.

such (sŭch) *adj.* of a certain kind
That was <u>such</u> a nice picnic.

summer (sŭm′ ər) *n.* the warm season of the year
I can't wait for <u>summer</u>!

Sunday (sŭn′ dē) *n.* the first day of the week
We went to church on <u>Sunday</u>.

sung (sŭng) *v.* past participle of *sing*
I did not know the song that was <u>sung</u> last night.

supper (sŭp′ ər) *n.* the last meal of the day; the evening meal
We had roast chicken for <u>supper</u> last night.

swallow

(swŏl′ ō) *n.* a small bird, very quick, with a forked tail
The <u>swallow</u> built a nest in our barn.
v. to let food or drink go down the throat into
the stomach
Bob could hardly <u>swallow</u> after his tonsils were
taken out.
swallow, swallows, swallowing, swallowed

swing

(swĭng) *n.* a seat or bar suspended from a brace
on which to move back and forth
Mom pushed the <u>swing</u> very high.
v. moving back and forth in the air
Sarah likes to <u>swing</u> high in the air.
swing, swings, swinging, swung

T

tail (tāl) *n.* part of an animal's body that
sticks out beyond the backbone
When my dog is glad to see me, he wags his <u>tail</u>.

tale (tāl) *n.* a story
Kate read us a fairy <u>tale</u>.

tan (tăn) *adj.* light brown
Midge had a <u>tan</u> coat.

tearful (tĭr′ fəl) *adj.* crying, sad
Max was <u>tearful</u> when his sister left.

tenth (tĕnth) *adj.* next in a series after the 9th
Do you know what the <u>tenth</u> commandment is?

tested (tĕst′ əd) *v.* past tense of *test*
John was <u>tested</u> on his reading skills.

thankful (thăngk′ fəl) *adj.* grateful
Betty was <u>thankful</u> for all the help she received.

Thanksgiving (thăngks gĭv′ ĭng) *n.* a special day in the United States
set aside to remember past blessings
We celebrate <u>Thanksgiving</u> Day in November.

theirs (therz) *pronoun.* possessive of *they*
Are the books on the table ours or <u>theirs</u>?

they'll	(thāl) *contraction.* they will Do you know when <u>they'll</u> be here?
they've	(thāv) *contraction.* they have <u>They've</u> been held up because of bad weather.
thimble	(thĭm′ b ə l) *n.* a small cap put on the finger to protect it; used in sewing Mom wears a <u>thimble</u> when she mends my jeans.
thing	(thĭng) *n.* an object or substance Only one <u>thing</u> is left to do before we can go.
think	(thĭngk) *v.* use the mind; ponder The last problem on my math test really made me <u>think</u>. think, thinks, thinking, thought
thinner	(thĭn′ ə r) *adj.* comparative of *thin* My pencil is <u>thinner</u> than yours.
thinnest	(thĭn′ ə st) *adj.* superlative of *thin* Please give me the <u>thinnest</u> slice of pizza.
thirteen	(thėr′ tēn′) *n.* number between 12 and 14 Jan's sister will be <u>thirteen</u> on Thursday.
thirty	(thėr′ tē) *n.* number 10 times 3 Jesus began to preach when he was <u>thirty</u>.

throne (thrōn) *n.* a special chair used by kings or officials
The king's <u>throne</u> was made of gold.

Thursday (thėrz′ dē) *n.* the 5th day of the week
Thanksgiving Day is the fourth <u>Thursday</u> in November.

tightrope (tīt′ rōp) *n.* a rope stretched tightly high above the ground
We saw a <u>tightrope</u> walker at the circus.

tile (tīl) *n.* a thin piece of baked clay, stone, or other material used for roofs, floors, or counter tops
We put new <u>tile</u> in our kitchen.
v. to put down tile
Dad wanted to <u>tile</u> the bathroom floor.
tile, tiles, tiling, tiled

tip (tĭp) *n.* the very end of something
The <u>tip</u> of the dog's tail was white.
v. to knock over
Be careful not to <u>tip</u> your glass and spill your juice.
tip, tips, tipping, tipped

tomorrow (tə môr′ ō) *adv.* the next day after today
I'll see you again <u>tomorrow</u> morning.

tonight (tə nīt′) *n.* this evening
Will you go to the game with me <u>tonight</u>?

took (tŭk) *v.* past tense of *take*
Who <u>took</u> my green hat?

tool (tül) *n.* an instrument needed to fix something
What <u>tool</u> will you need to fix the chair?

top (tŏp) *n.* an object that spins
The baby liked to watch the <u>top</u> spinning.
adj. the highest point
We climbed to the <u>top</u> floor of the building.

torches (tôrch′ əz) *n.* plural of *torch;* a light that can
be carried or stuck in a wall holder
After dark, they lit <u>torches</u> so that we could see.

tougher (tŭf′ ər) *adj.* comparative of *tough*
This trail is <u>tougher</u> than the one we hiked before.

toughest (tŭf′ əst) *adj.* superlative of *tough*
That was the <u>toughest</u> math test I've ever taken!

town (toun) *n.* a small city; a place where people live
and work
Our <u>town</u> has a new post office.

trail (trāl) *n.* a path
The mountain <u>trail</u> is very steep.

train (trān) *n.* a line of railroad cars
Ben will take the <u>train</u> to see his grandparents.
v. to teach someone how to do something
Jenny will <u>train</u> the dog to sit.
train, trains, training, trained

true

(trü) *adj.* exact; according to the facts
Do you think that story was <u>true</u>?

trust

(trŭst) *n.* belief in the honesty of a person or thing
You can place your <u>trust</u> in God.
v. to depend on or put faith in
The motto or our country is, "In God we <u>trust</u>."
trust, trusts, trusting, trusted

truthful

(trüth′ fə l) *adj.* honest
I can always count on Ben to be <u>truthful</u>.

tub

(tŭb) *n.* a large container
that can hold water
Please fill the <u>tub</u> with water.

Tuesday

(tüz′ dē) *n.* the 3rd day of the week
Jim will arrive on <u>Tuesday</u>.

tug

(tŭg) *v.* to pull hard; to pull with effort
Brian had to <u>tug</u> on the door to get it to close.
tug, tugs, tugging, tugged

twelve

(twĕlv) *adj.* being one more than eleven
Jesus chose <u>twelve</u> apostles.

twenty

(twĕn′ tē) *adj.* number ten times two
Grant needed <u>twenty</u> people to help him.

U

undo (ŭn dü′) *v.* untie, unfasten
Can you <u>undo</u> this knot for me?
undo, undid, undoing, undone

uneasy (ŭn ē′ zē) *adj.* not comfortable with
Mark felt <u>uneasy</u> about going to
the barber for the first time.

uneven (ŭn ē′ vən) *adj.* not level or even
The sidewalk was <u>uneven</u>.

unfair (ŭn fer′) *adj.* not just or fair
It was <u>unfair</u> of Jack not to call you.

United States (yü nī′ təd stāts′) *n.* country made up of 50 states,
mostly in North America
Carlos moved to the <u>United States</u> from Peru.

unjust (ŭn jŭst′) *adj.* not fair or right
Martin was <u>unjust</u> in accusing Bill without any proof.

unkind (ŭn kīnd′) *adj.* hurtful, not kind
The man was very <u>unkind</u> to the little boy.

unlike (ŭn līk′) *adj.* not the same, different
That house is <u>unlike</u> any other I've seen.

unload   (ŭn lōd´) *v.* remove, or take out of
         Can you help me <u>unload</u> the groceries from the car?
         unload, unloads, unloading, unloaded

unlock   (ŭn lŏk´) *v.* to open
         Can you please <u>unlock</u> the door for me?
         unlock, unlocks, unlocking, unlocked

unpack   (ŭn păk) *v.* to empty out
         I helped Bob <u>unpack</u> his suitcase.
         unpack, unpacks, unpacking, unpacked

used   (yüzd) *v.* past tense of *use*
         Martha <u>used</u> her new recipe for supper.

useful   (yüs´ fəl) *adj.* good, helpful
         This book was very <u>useful</u>.

V

valentine (văl´ ən tīn) *n.* a special card or gift sent on Valentine's Day
Mark sent me a <u>valentine</u>.

verb (vėrb) *n.* a part of speech expressing action
The word *run* is an action <u>verb</u>.

verse (vėrs) *n.* a section or group of lines from a song, poem, psalm, etc.
Can you recite a <u>verse</u> from Psalm 50?

W

wait (wāt) *v.* to remain still; stay in one place
Please <u>wait</u> your turn.

waited (wāt´ əd) *v.* past tense of *wait*
We <u>waited</u> three hours to see the doctor.

wanted (wŏnt´ əd) *v.* past tense of *want*
Sue and Ken <u>wanted</u> to come with us.

watches (wŏch´ əz) *n.* plural of *watch*
Sam had three new <u>watches</u>.

water   (wô′ tər) *n.* colorless liquid that fills lakes and rivers
The <u>water</u> on the lake shone in the sunlight.
v. to give water to something
Please <u>water</u> the garden today.
water, waters, watering, watered

wax   (wăks) *n.* a substance used to make candles or a paste
for shining floors, cars, furniture
The <u>wax</u> from the candle dripped on the table.
v. to put wax on something
Dad and I will wash and <u>wax</u> the car today.
wax, waxes, waxing, waxed

waxes   (wăks′ əz) *v.* present tense of *wax*
John <u>waxes</u> his car every week.

we   (wē) *pronoun.* persons speaking together
When will <u>we</u> get our new car?

Wednesday   (wĕnz′ dē) *n.* the 4th day of the week
We're going swimming on <u>Wednesday</u>.

wee   (wē) *adj.* very tiny
A <u>wee</u> little rabbit ran into the hole.

weren't   (wėrnt) *contraction.* were not
Pam and Brenda <u>weren't</u> in class today.

we've   (wēv) *contraction.* we have
When <u>we've</u> finished, we'll call you.

wheat   (hwēt) *n.* a grass that produces seed
used to make flour
There were fields of <u>wheat</u> as
far as the eye could see.

while   (hwīl) *conj.* a space of time
Please watch the dog <u>while</u> I'm gone.

whisper   (hwĭs' pər) *n.* a very soft tone of voice
Speak in a <u>whisper</u>, the baby's sleeping.
v. to speak very low and softly
Marge had to <u>whisper</u> so she wouldn't disturb the
others.
whisper, whispers, whispering, whispered

whose   (hüz) *adj.* to whom something belongs
Do you know <u>whose</u> shoes these are?

why   (hwī) *adv.* what reason
Did you ask Carl <u>why</u> he was late?

win   (wĭn) *v.* to come in first, to get a prize
The best team will <u>win</u> the trophy.
win, wins, winning, won

wing   (wĭng) *n.* a structure attached to the side of a bird
or a plane that allows it to fly
The sparrow had a broken <u>wing</u>.

winter

(wĭn′ t ə r) *n.* the cold season of the year
We will go sledding this <u>winter</u>.

wish

(wĭsh) *n.* a desire or hope for something
Make a <u>wish</u> before you blow out the candles!
v. to want or desire something
I <u>wish</u> that I could go see Grandma this week.
wish, wishes, wishing, wished

wishes

(wĭsh′ ə z) *n.* plural of *wish*
How many <u>wishes</u> did you make?

without

(wĭth out′) *preposition.* not having something; free from
Jill left <u>without</u> her umbrella.

wonderful

(wŭn′ d ə r f ə l) *adj.* amazing
The party was a <u>wonderful</u> surprise.

won't

(wōnt) *contraction.* will not
Nate said that he <u>won't</u> be able to drive us to the game.

wood

(wo͝od) *n.* material from trees used for building and for fires
Tom gathered <u>wood</u> for the fire.

wool

(wo͝ol) *n.* soft, curly hair of sheep and some other animals
The sheep had thick, soft <u>wool</u>.

word   (wėrd) *n.* a letter or group of letters that has meaning
What <u>word</u> did you misspell?

work   (wėrk) *n.* something to be done
We still have a lot of <u>work</u> to do on this project
v. to do something
We will <u>work</u> on the lawn this afternoon.
work, works, working, worked

world   (wėrld) *n.* the earth
Jesus takes away the sins of the <u>world</u>.

wouldn't   (wůd′ nt) *contraction.* would not
Kathy <u>wouldn't</u> like that dress.

wow   (wou) *interjection.* surprise, delight
<u>Wow</u>!! Look at all the gifts!

71

X

xylophone   (zī′ lə fōn) *n.* a musical instrument with two rows of wooden or metal bars of different lengths that make a musical tone when struck
Jim played the <u>xylophone</u> in the school band.

Y

yak   (yăk) *n.* a long-haired animal found in the mountains of Asia
Do you know another name for a <u>yak</u>?

yam   (yăm) *n.* an orange-colored root vegetable
Mary ate a baked <u>yam</u> for supper.

yell   (yĕl) *v.* shout
Please don't <u>yell</u> so loud!
yell, yells, yelling, yelled

you've   (yüv) *contraction.* you have
<u>You've</u> got to have your toys picked up before supper.

"Working Words" Word List

A

C

E

G

H

J

K

83

L

M

N

O

R

S

U-V

X-Y-Z

Cumulative Word List - Spelling 1 & 2

A

a	after	along	and	arm	August
about	afternoon	alphabet	ant	around	aunt
ache	airplane	always	anyone	ask	ax
across	airport	am	April	asked	axes
add	all	an	are	ate	

B

baby	bed	beside	black	boot	brother
back	bedroom	best	blame	both	brown
ball	been	better	blend	bottle	bubble
bare	bees	between	bless	bowl	burn
baseball	before	beyond	blow	box	but
batter	began	big	blue	boxes	butter
be	begging	bigger	bluff	boy	butterfly
beaches	behind	biggest	boat	boy's	by
bear	believe	bind	boil	brave	
became	bell	bird	bone	bread	
because	below	birthday	book	break	
become	belt	bitter	books	breakfast	

97

C

cage	cent	Christ	classes	come	cross
called	center	Christian	clay	cook	cry
calling	chick	Christmas	click	cooked	cuff
came	child	church	climb	cool	cupful
can	children	circus	clock	cooled	curb
can't	child's	circle	clothes	cot	cut
cape	children's	city	cloud	cough	cute
car	chill	clang	clown	could	
cat	chime	clasp	cob	couldn't	
cattle	chin	class	cold	count	

D

daddy	deer	dirt	does	down	duck
day	did	dishes	dolls	dream	
dear	didn't	do	don't	dresses	
December	dinner	dock	door	drop	

E

each	eat	eighteen	eleven	enlarge	eye
early	echo	eighth	enclose	entire	
earth	eggs	eighty	enjoy	entrust	
Easter	eight	elephant	enjoyment	every	

F

farm	fifty	float	forget	fox	frog
faster	find	flower	forgetful	foxes	from
fastest	first	fly	forgot	foxhole	fur
fearless	five	foam	forty	free	
February	fix	food	found	Friday	
feet	flake	foot	four	friend	
fifteen	flame	football	fourteen	friendship	
fifth	flew	for	fourth	fries	

G

gas	gift	glass	gnome	goose	guess
gate	girl	globe	go	gopher	gum
geese	giggle	glue	goat	grade	
gentle	ginger	gnash	God	grateful	
get	girl's	gnat	good	green	
giant	glad	gnaw	goodness	grow	

H

hammer	hard	he'll	high	hop	house
handful	have	helpful	higher	hope	houses
hands	haven't	helpless	highest	hopeless	how
hang	he	hem	hiked	hoping	huddle
happier	head	her	him	hopped	huge
happiest	headache	here	his	hopping	hugged
happiness	hear	hers	home	hot	hugging
happy	he'd	hide	hood	hour	hundred

I

I	I'd	I'm	inside	it's	it
ice	I'll	in	its	I've	itch

J

January	join	joy	judgment	July	just
Jesus	joke	joyful	juggle	June	

K

kettle	kindness	kneel	knight	know
kind	kites	knees	knives	knows
kinder	kneads	knew	knock	known
kindest	knee	knife	knot	

L

lad	learn	life	littlest	longest	luck
ladder	leg	light	lives	look	lunch
lamb	lemon	like	loaded	looked	lunches
lass	less	lip	lock	looking	lung
latch	letter	little	long	love	
laugh	lick	littler	longer	low	

M

made	match	meek	mile	mommy	mother
mail	math	meet	mine	Monday	mouth
mailman	May	melted	miss	moon	Mr.
make	me	men	mix	moonlight	Mrs.
many	meal	met	mixed	mop	much
map	meat	mice	mixes	morning	must
March	meatloaf	middle	mom	most	my

N

needs	nibble	nineteen	nod	not	nurse
nerve	nice	ninety	noise	November	
never	night	ninth	noon	now	
new	nine	no	nose	nowhere	

O

October	old	one	other	outside	ox
off	on	or	out	over	oxen

P

pack	peace	phone	plan	pond	puppies
paddle	peaches	phonics	plant	pool	purple
page	peak	photo	plate	praise	purse
park	peek	photograph	play	pray	puzzle
part	pen	pick	played	prayed	
patch	pencil	pie	playful	present	
patchwork	people	pine	please	prettiest	
path	pet	pitch	plow	pretty	
Paul	pets	pizza	poke	puddle	

Q

quack	quest	quiet	quilt	quiz
queen	quick	quietly	quit	

R

rabbit	rattle	rich	road	rope	rubber
rain	reaches	riddle	rock	rough	run
rainbow	read	right	rode	roughly	rung
rang	reed	ring	roof	row	

sack	second	shook	slow	somehow	story
saddle	see	short	small	someone	stove
said	seek	should	smaller	something	stranger
sail	seen	shouldn't	smallest	song	straw
sang	September	shout	smart	south	street
sat	serve	sick	smell	speak	string
Saturday	seven	sight	smile	spell	stripe
saw	seventeen	sign	smiling	spelling	strong
say	seventh	sing	smoke	splash	stronger
scarf	seventy	sip	snack	spoon	strongest
scarves	shall	sir	snail	spray	such
scene	she	sixteen	snake	squeak	summer
scent	she's	sixth	snow	stay	Sunday
school	sheep	sixty	snuggle	stem	sung
science	shell	skate	so	stick	supper
scissors	shine	skip	soap	stir	swallow
scribble	ship	skirt	sock	stone	swing
script	shirt	sky	softer	stood	
scrub	shoe	sleep	softest	stop	
sea	shoeless	slip	some	store	

T

tail	that	think	tightrope	top	trust
tale	the	thinner	tile	torches	truthful
tall	their	thinnest	time	toss	trying
tan	theirs	third	tip	tough	tub
tax	then	thirteen	toe	tougher	tube
tearful	they	thirty	tomorrow	toughest	Tuesday
ten	they'll	this	tonight	town	tug
tenth	they've	three	to	toy	turn
tested	thick	throne	too	trail	twelve
thank	thimble	throw	took	train	twenty
thankful	thin	Thursday	tool	tree	two
Thanksgiving	thing	tie	tooth	true	

U

under	unfair	unlike	until	used
undo	United States	unload	up	useful
uneasy	unjust	unlock	us	
uneven	unkind	unpack	use	

V

valentine   verb   verse   very

W

wait	wax	weren't	whisper	winter	word
waited	waxes	we've	white	wish	work
walk	we	whale	who	wishes	world
walls	weak	what	whole	with	wouldn't
wanted	Wednesday	wheat	whose	without	wow
was	wee	when	why	wonderful	write
watch	well	where	will	won't	
watches	went	which	win	wood	
water	were	while	wing	wool	

X-Y-Z

x-ray	yak	yawn	yellow	you	you're
xylophone	yam	yell	yes	your	you've